acrylics

by Mari Bolte

illustrated by D.C. Ice

Content Consultant:
Robert A. Williams
Artist and Teacher
Instructor of Commercial and Technical Art
South Central College, North Mankato, Minnesota

CAPSTONE PRESS
a capstone imprint

Snap Books are published by Capstone Press,
1710 Roe Crest Drive, North Mankato, Minnesota 56003.
www.capstonepub.com

Library of Congress Cataloging-in-Publication Data
Bolte, Mari.
  Acrylics / By Mari Bolte ; illustrated by D.C. Ice.
     pages cm. — (Snap books. Paint it)
  Summary: "Step-by-step guides show how to create a variety of projects using
acrylic paints"—Provided by publisher.
  ISBN 978-1-4765-3109-0 (library binding)
  ISBN 978-1-4765-3567-8 (ebook PDF)
1. Acrylic painting—Technique—Juvenile literature. I. Title.
  ND1535.B65 2014
  751.42'6—dc23
                                              2013005395

Designer: Bobbie Nuytten
Production Specialist: Laura Manthe

Photo Credits:
Illustrations by D.C. Ice; all photos by Capstone Studio and
D.C. Ice except the following: The Art and Creative Materials Institute,
Inc. (ACMI), 6 (seals), Shutterstock: aldegonde, 18 (bottom),
Andreka, 14 (top), Cathy Keifer, 22 (middle left), konmesa, 28 (top),
woldswildlifewonders, 21 (top left)

Printed in the United States of America in Stevens Point, Wisconsin.
032013   007227WZF13

Table of Contents

IN YOUR ART BOX

Acrylic paint knows no limits! You can use it to paint a masterpiece or create crafts. Put paintbrush to paint and decorate in the world in acrylics.

ACRYLIC PAINTS

When compared to other painting mediums, acrylics are new to the art world. They first appeared in the 1940s.

Although acrylic paints resemble oils, there are things that set them apart. Acrylic paints use a binder called acrylic resin. This resin dries quickly and is still flexible. Used alone, acrylic resin can be used as a glue. Acrylic paints can be thinned with mineral spirits or water.

Pigments used for oil paintings can be used for acrylic paints too. The amount of pigment used can change the way the paint looks. Less pigment can give your paints the look of watercolors. Add more and they will look like oils.

Paints and Pigments

All paints are made up of a pigment and a binder. Pigments are dry, colored powders. They can be natural or artificial, and can come from plants, animals, the earth, or a lab. Pigment is what colors all painting mediums. The only difference between paint mediums is the binder that is used.

Binders are adhesive liquids that hold pigment. Pigment reacts differently depending on the binder that is used. This is why one color of oil paint looks different than the same color of watercolor paint.

PAPERS

Use acrylic paint anywhere!
Paper, cardstock, wood, or canvas are common surfaces.

You can buy paper specifically designed for acrylic paints.
These sheets of paper resemble actual canvas. You can also
buy panels mounted with pieces of canvas. The canvas will be
pre-primed, which will help your paintings last longer.

BRUSHES AND KNIVES

A variety of brushes means a variety of textures and strokes in your art. Buy the best brushes you can afford, even if you're just starting out. A good basic set includes three round brushes of various sizes, a detail round, and a full-belly round.

Brushes used for acrylic painting need to be soaked during use. This keeps the paints in the brush bristles from drying out. Natural-bristle brushes can lose their shape if soaked often. Synthetic brushes might be a better choice if you plan on doing a lot of acrylic painting.

Dried acrylic paint is very difficult to remove from brush bristles. Soaking in strong solvents might remove the paint. However, the solvents can also damage the brush.

Go beyond brushes and try out a painting knife. Painting knives are used to apply paint. Palette knives are used for cleaning your palette. Spatulas and scrapers can be used to mix paint. You can also use them to scrape paint onto your painting. Start with a basic, quality painting knife made of tempered steel. If you like what it does, you can always buy more.

Palette knives come in a variety of shapes and sizes.

TIPS AND TECHNIQUES

Practice your brush strokes to find the techniques that work best for you. Try:

~**Tape Masking** Use tape to create designs on paper. Paint over the tape. Remove once paint is dry. Create multiple layers, if desired.

~**Hard and Soft Edges** Practice blocking in color to create hard and soft edges. Experiment with old credit cards, stencils, stamps, and palette knives for hard edges. Rags, thick bristle brushes, and water are good for soft edges.

~**Scumbling** Apply paint in a cross-hatch pattern to experiment with scumbling

~**Wet Paint** Try thinning the paint with water. Apply your watery paint in drips or splashes.

Tape Masking

Hard-edge & Soft-edge

Cross-hatch Brush Stroke

Stay Safe!

The Art and Creative Materials Institute (ACMI) tests art supplies. They make sure paints are properly labeled.

Supplies with the AP seal from ACMI are certified nontoxic. Nontoxic items will not cause major health problems in people.

Supplies with the CL label do potentially contain toxic or hazardous materials. However, with appropriate handling they can be used safely. Directions on the container or package should be followed exactly.

ACMI
ART & CREATIVE MATERIALS INSTITUTE CERTIFIED
AP ®
Conforms to
ASTM D 4236

ACMI
ART & CREATIVE MATERIALS INSTITUTE CERTIFIED
CL ®
Conforms to
ASTM D 4236

~**Sgraffito** Scrape off wet or dry paint with a palette knife or other sharp item.

~**Dry Brush** Practice various brush strokes with a dry brush to see how they look in layers.

~**Stencils and Stamps** Use stencils and stamps to create texture and patterns. Your fingers are the perfect natural stamp!

~**Wet And Dry** Apply wet paint to wet paper. Also try using a very wet brush on dry paper.

Sgraffito Technique

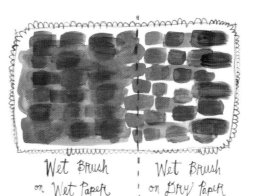

Wet Brush on Wet Paper | *Wet Brush on Dry Paper*

Acrylic paint dries quickly. Thickly applied areas of paint need only a day or two to dry.

Stencil & Stamp Painting

Dry Brush

COLOR PALETTE

Acrylic paints come in many premixed colors. However, most artists start with a base palette of between eight and 12 main colors. Below is a list containing some of the more common colors:

Lemon Yellow, Azo Yellow Medium, Cadmium Red Light, Permanent Rose, Permanent Alizarin Crimson, Ultramarine Blue, Phthalo Blue Green Shade, Phthalo Green Blue Shade, Raw Umber, Yellow Ochre, Burnt Sienna, and Titanium White.

Apply Paint with a Card

Some pigments are toxic. If you're not sure whether a pigment is toxic, check the label. Many toxic pigments have a metal in their name, such as copper, cadmium, cobalt, and lead.

Finger Painting

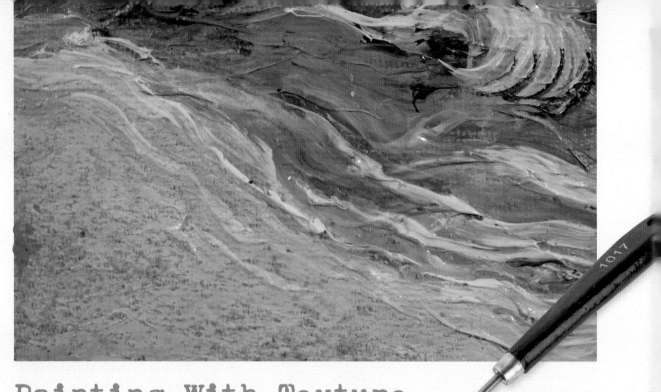

Painting With Texture

Thick layers of paint create swirling white waves and sandy beaches. This technique, called impasto, gives an almost 3D feel. Create this tropical texture by painting with palette knives and gel medium.

1. Apply paint thickly to the canvas. Use the back of a palette knife to paint the sky and the beach.

2. Try a variety of palette knives to paint the water. Experiment with dabbing, layering, and adding swirls. Alternate between using white and shades of blue.

3. Use the tip of a palette knife to add palm trees. Apply the paint with the flat part. Use the edges and tip to create the leaves on the tree.

4. Mix sand with the paint you use to paint the beach. Add the sandy paint in multiple layers.

Use a thick gel medium to give your waves more texture.

Gel medium is an unpigmented acrylic liquid. It extends the drying time for acrylic paint. It can be used to smooth out or thicken paint. It can also be used like glue.

BASICS
gloss fluid medium
use with acrylic paint
medium liquide brillant
medio fluido brillante
250ml ℮ 8.79 US. fl.oz

Make sure your palette knife is not too sharp. A sharp knife can cut right through your canvas (or your skin!) If your knife is too sharp, it can be dulled by rubbing the edge with sandpaper.

Dark to Light Abstract

Layers of flat paint can have just as much depth as impasto paintings. Start with a plain black canvas. Shed some light with increasingly light circles. Make colors pop with a splash of yellow.

Acrylic paint dries quickly. Squeeze out small amount of paints to minimize waste.

1 Paint a white canvas all black. Let dry.

2 Fill the canvas with dark blue circles.

3 Add a bit of white paint to the blue before painting more circles. Vary the circles' sizes and positions.

4 Continue adding white circles until your top layer is nearly covered.

5 Add yellow circles.

6 Add gold circles.

7 Don't stop now. Add as many layers as you want. Try going backward, adding more dark blue paint to the white.

Try applying paint without brushes. Rags, sponges, or your fingers are great alternatives!

11

Color Test

Experiment with color! Create a grid
and test out different color and shape
combinations. Outline your squares with
black to make them look like stained glass.

*Quilting patterns are
another great inspiration
for geometric shapes.*

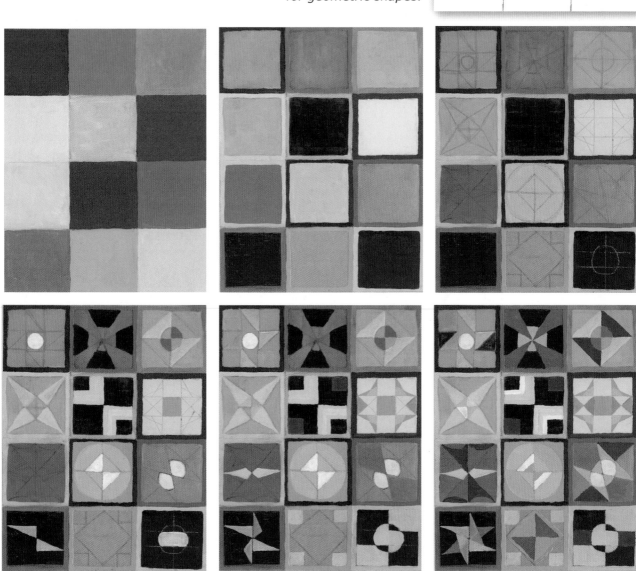

1 Use a ruler to draw even squares on your canvas.

2 Paint each square a different color. Let dry.

3 Use a pencil to lightly sketch geometric shapes into each square.

4 Paint each of the geometric shapes you drew. Let dry.

5 Turn your shapes into stained glass by outlining all the edges with black marker.

Flat-edged brushes work best for putting fine lines on your geometric shapes.

Match the Shade

Acrylic paint dries two shades darker. Keep that in mind when mixing wet paint for this project.

You don't need a huge rainbow of color to create vivid paintings. Pick a picture to recreate. Identify the base colors used in that image. Then stick to them.

1 Use painting tape to mask off a square of your canvas paper.

2 Draw light grid lines to help map out the placement of the balloons. Draw the balloons in pencil.

3 Using only the two shades of pink, paint the balloons.

4 Paint the sky using only the two shades of blue.

5 Create the clouds using the light blue paint. Use a small fan brush to soften the clouds' edges.

6 Use a thin liner brush to add the balloon strings.

Color-Field

Color-Fields

Color-fields were first painted in the 1950s. Artists wanted to create pieces that were modern, abstract, and bright. See works by Helen Frankenthaler, Kenneth Nolan, and Morris Louis.

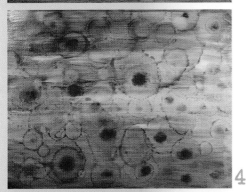

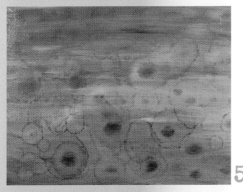

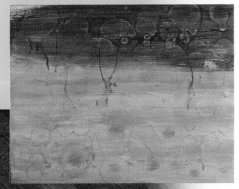

New artists sometimes have a hard time filling the whole canvas. Get over your fears by creating a huge color-field.

1 Paint your canvas any color you want. Be sure to fill the entire space. Let dry.

2 Choose another color. Use a small plastic cup to mix two parts water to one part paint.

3 Use a large, fat-ended brush to coat the entire canvas with the watered-down paint. Do not let dry.

4 Drip alcohol onto the canvas before the paint dries. The alcohol will repel the watery paint and let the base layer of paint show through.

5 Let the alcohol and water paint dry. Continue adding as many layers of watery paint and alcohol as you want.

For more layering, drip watery paint in different colors onto the canvas. Allow paint to run together and blend before adding the alcohol.

17

Blackout

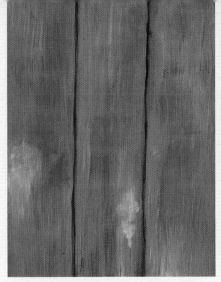

Did you notice that black wasn't in the Color Palette list at the beginning of the book? That's because you can make your own! Black from a tube can overpower your other paints. You can get a more diverse black depending on which colors you mix.

1 Test and compare different color blends, including:
~Prussian Blue/Burnt Sienna
~Raw Umber/Prussian Blue
~Burnt Umber/Ultramarine Blue

Test out and compare different color blends. Each black will be subtly different.

2 Once you've tested each color combination, mix each with a bit with white. This will show the color mixture's undertone.

3 After you're done experimenting, challenge yourself! Pick a picture to paint in black and white—without using true black.

4 Roughly layer different colors to create the wooden fence's texture.

5 Paint the shape of the skates.

6 Add details to the skates, including the laces, stitching, and blades.

Burnt Sienna | Prussian Blue   Raw Umber | Prussian Blue   Burnt Umber | Ultramarine Blue   Black

Mix your paints on your palette thoroughly.

Eye on Perspective

Animal eyes come in all shapes, sizes, and colors. Stare them down and study them closely! Focus on light, colors, and details to make these eyes as real as possible.

Keep your fine-tip brushes free of excess paint. This will ensure clean lines in your detail work.

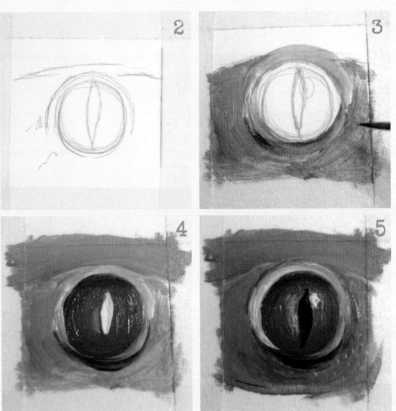

1 Use painter's tape to mask off even squares across your canvas.

2 Draw a rough sketch of an eye in each square.

3 Begin by painting the area around the eye. Add general color tones. You will go back and paint small details later.

4 Paint the actual eye. Work with the main base color. Then add color and shading to give the eye a rounded shape. Paint dark-to-light, bottom-to-top for the most natural feel.

5 Use small-tipped brushes to add highlights to the area around the eye. Blend paint to add light and shadows.

continued on next page

Find close-up photographs of animal eyes to use for reference. Nature magazines, Internet searches, and other websites like Pinterest will help you find vivid shots.

Master the eye before attempting the rest of the animal. A beautiful eye will help your wildlife seem alive.

6 Once paint is dry, carefully peel off tape.

7 Carefully cut out each square. Leave a border around each square, if desired. To skip the cutting step, paint your eyes on artist trading cards.

8 Laminate or varnish each square for extra protection.

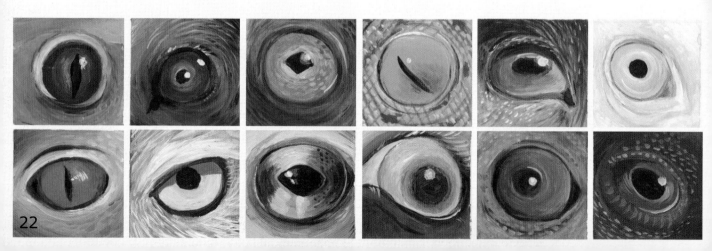

Mayan Art

continued on next page

Use the sgraffito technique to scratch out Mayan-inspired art. Use household items to scratch away layers of paint and expose colorful underlayers.

1 Paint a circle with acrylic paint. Let dry.

2 Mix white paint with an equal amount of gel medium.

3 Paint a bird in the middle of the circle. Do not allow paint to dry.

4 Quickly use a key to scrape long and short lines off the bird's wings and body.

5 Mix black paint with gel medium. Paint the space above the bird. Do not allow paint to dry.

6 Use a nail to draw lines into the black paint. Scratch hard enough to allow color underneath to show through.

7 Add details to the bird, such as beak and chest feathers.

8 Mix red paint with gel medium. Paint the space below the bird. Do not allow paint to dry.

9 Use a pencil eraser to scratch the star and moon into the red paint.

10 Draw zigzags around the circle with red and yellow paint. Let dry.

11 Mix light gray with gel medium. Paint a large circle over and around the yellow and red zigzags.

12 Use an old toothbrush to push the gray paint out, toward the edges of the circle.

13 Use the pencil eraser to scratch over the zigzag pattern. This will expose the red paint underneath.

14 Paint around the zigzag with black paint.

15 Mix red and yellow paint with gel medium. Paint around the whole image one last time. Do not let dry.

16 Use a hair comb to scratch waves around the outer layer.

Some gel mediums come premixed with glass, pumice, or small pieces of acrylic. These give the gel different properties, such as a shiny surface or a rough texture. Try using one or all of these gels for added effect.

Fantasy Art

Have you ever looked out your window and wished your view was of something different? Grab a paintbrush, buy a window to paint, and make it happen! Bring your dream view to life with this fantasy art project.

If you can't find a window, use a sheet of clear acrylic. Both windows and acrylic sheets can be found at home improvement stores.

1 Wash the window thoroughly. Make sure all traces of window cleaner have been removed.

2 If you're worried about painting onto the wood, mask the edges of the window with painter's tape.

3 Think about what you want to paint. Planning ahead is important for this project. Mistakes can be corrected, but fixes can take time.

4 Dip a round-tipped brush into pink paint. Then dip it into red paint. Then dip it into orange paint. This will create a layered effect as you paint the flowers.

5 Swirl the paint onto the glass. The layered paint will blend together. Add as many flowers as you wish. Let dry.

6 Paint green vines and leaves for the flowers.

Varnish

Most acrylic paintings should be varnished. Varnish protects your paintings from light damage, humidity, and dust. It is sold in spray cans and as a liquid to brush on.

Apply varnish outdoors or in a well-ventilated room. Allow your paint to dry between 48 and 72 hours before adding varnish.

If using brush-on varnish, apply in one to three thin, even coats. Overlap each brush stroke slightly. Do not go back over wet varnish. This can cause a cloudy appearance. Allow at least 12 hours before applying another coat.

7 Add a fence to the background. Let dry completely.

8 Paint the birds and any remaining flower details.

9 To protect your art, you'll need to seal the paint. This is especially important because paint can be scratched or washed off glass. Acrylic varnish works best. Follow the safety tips in the sidebar above.

> *To fix a mistake, press a paper towel dipped in window cleaner onto the paint. Then use a razor blade to gently scrape paint off the glass.*

Painting Wildlife

Zoom out and take your eye study and color matching skills to the next level. Pick a photo, trace your tiger, and get painting!

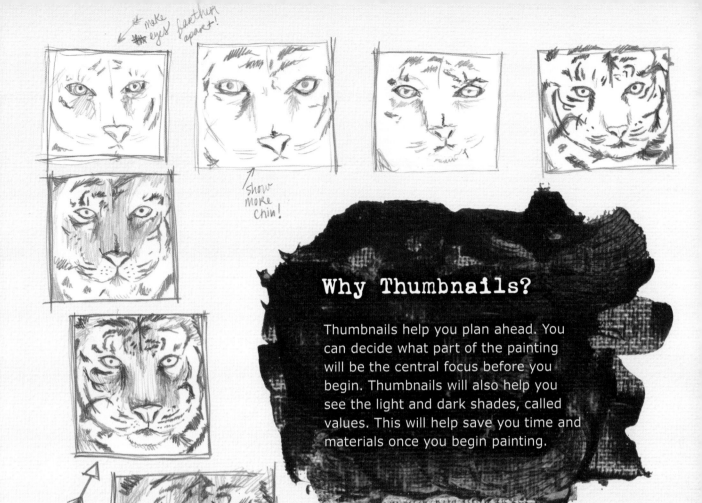

make # eyes farther apart!

show more chin!

Why Thumbnails?

Thumbnails help you plan ahead. You can decide what part of the painting will be the central focus before you begin. Thumbnails will also help you see the light and dark shades, called values. This will help save you time and materials once you begin painting.

3

1 Paint a masonite board with cream-colored paint. Let dry.

2 Select a photo. Use it to create at least two thumbnail sketches. The two thumbnails should have different focal points and values.

3 Draw the picture of the tiger onto tracing paper. Try to capture the values chosen in the thumbnail.

continued on next page

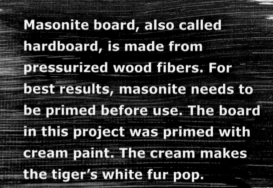

Masonite board, also called hardboard, is made from pressurized wood fibers. For best results, masonite needs to be primed before use. The board in this project was primed with cream paint. The cream makes the tiger's white fur pop.

4 Turn the tracing paper over. Rub the back of the paper with an even layer of graphite.

5 Flip the paper back over. Place the tiger image over the masonite board. Use a pencil to trace over your drawing and transfer it onto the board.

6 Use a fan brush to create the tiger's white fur.

7 Add the tiger's black stripes.

8 Start with burnt orange paint. Blend until you have a shade of orange that matches your tiger.

9 Begin painting the tiger's orange parts. Start with the larger spaces first and work your way into the more detailed areas.

Start with the white areas first. This will help the orange blend naturally.

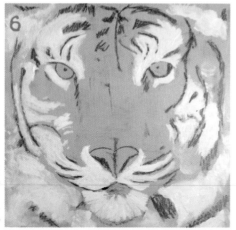

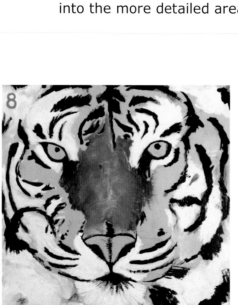

10

11

10 Continue layering orange paint of various shades and tones until tiger is completely painted.

11 Paint the tiger's eyes and nose. Start with the dark pupil. Add color in layers to give the eye a more lifelike feel.

12 Use a liner brush to paint the tiger's whiskers.

Go back and touch your tiger up where necessary. Add light strokes of white paint to mimic layers of fur.

12

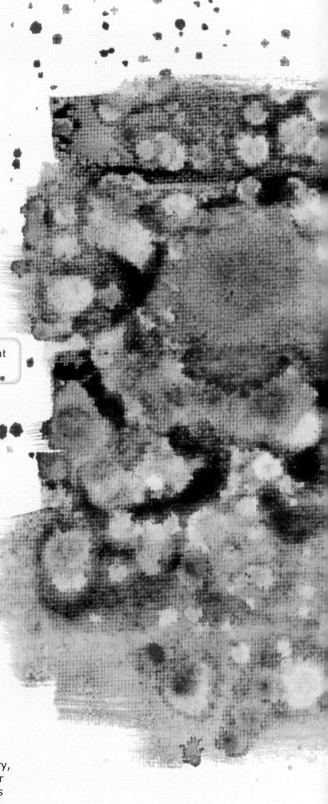

Read More

Frisch-Schmoll, Joy. *Portraits*. Brushes with Greatness. Mankato, Minn.: Creative Paperbacks, 2013.

Heine, Florian. *13 Painters Children Should Know*. New York: Prestel, 2012.

Runyen, Amy, and the Creative Team at Walter Foster. *You Can Paint Like the Masters*. Irvine, Calif.: Walter Foster, 2010.

Internet Sites

FactHound offers a safe, fun way to find Internet sites related to this book. All of the sites on FactHound have been researched by our staff.

Here's all you do:

Visit *www.facthound.com*

Type in this code: 9781476531090

 Check out projects, games and lots more at
www.capstonekids.com

Author Bio

Mari Bolte is an author of children's books and a lover of art. She lives in southern Minnesota with her husband, daughter, and two wiener dogs. A degree in creative writing has taught her the value of fine writing. Parenthood has made her a purveyor of fine art, with specializations in sidewalk chalk, washable markers, and glitter glue.

Illustrator Bio

D.C. Ice has more than a decade of experience as an illustrator of children's books and as an accomplished artist, with an emphasis on painting. Edgy animals with human attributes are the stars of her illustrations and paintings. As a member of a gallery in St. Paul, Minnesota, and a frequent exhibitor in multiple galleries throughout the country, her love of all things art continues to grow. D.C. received her Bachelor's Degree in Fine Arts from the College of Visual Arts in St. Paul.